# The Navigation of Butterflies

Kamryn Sanderfer

India | USA | UK

The Navigation of Butterflies © 2023
Kamryn Sanderfer

All rights reserved.

No part of this publication may be reproduced, stored in a retrieval system, or transmitted, in any form or by any means, electronic, mechanical, photocopying, recording or otherwise, without the prior written permission of the presenters.

Kamryn Sanderfer asserts the moral right to be identified as the author of this work.

Presentation by *BookLeaf Publishing*

Web: www.bookleafpub.com

E-mail: info@bookleafpub.com

ISBN: 9789358369274

First edition 2023

# DEDICATION

To God, for being worth it all.

# letter-writing desk

With fatigue, I write a letter
On paper with sharp corners
There may be a prick of my skin
As my arm skims the page
And it is my blood leaking through the pen
Writing words like taut, swooping heartstrings

With fatigue, I write a letter
On this desk of grainy wood
Chopped down through sweat and forest gore
Weeping from the loss
And then sanded into letter-writing desks

It is with fatigue that I write this letter
Because it is too much
While I am too small
So here is the letter
That lays it all down

# By the Back Window

Cold milk beads on the lip of my cup
Through a back window lies the green
And yellow
Of beginning
And there I sit, unaware.

# mad and mind

From the mountains of Chicago
To the flatlands of Calgary
I run from the purple,
teeming clouds of memory
Between the gaps I daydream
of valley and climbing vine
The mountains greet me there,
seagulls rest in snowy pine
But what's behind swirls near
mesmerizing me in fear
I am left and right and inside
the salt
of curls and waves and tears
I do not trust what I see,
I have lost that understanding
in the dizziness of spinning
but I must remain unceasing
In search
of something green.

# Mud

Mornings escape the summer heat
I sleep with the dew on beds of green
Coffee is still bitter, his breath still sweet
In the backyard
The mud on my skin is not a stain
and neither is love,
and neither is pain

# false light

Light at the end of the tunnel,
now shadow I carry in my pocket
and in my head
where thoughts swim in reggae tunes
taunting
and the waves are choppy, I
am left behind
My teeth grind in the grit
and it is you
that I can't spit out.

# Glittering Youth

Youth hides behind a golden veil,
tempting with its glittering ripple
like sunshine on the lake water
behind your old best friend's house
where laughter was consumed by the wind
and each other's voices,
talking about things that don't really matter,
like the shadows in the basement
that were only shadows.

# getting tired

will I always be this way
shuddering with the past
scizzors in my hair
and a sickness in my stomach
with endless questions
I don't want answered?

# The Good Man

We were united by butterflies
They left their powdery designs behind
On our fingers, and in our nets
As we walked
And he was quiet,
gentle.
We then went 'round the block
Running shoes on cracked sidewalk
Blinking in the sun
As we ran
And he was quiet,
softly
When we went to the ocean, gray and cold
Swimming, choking, later laughing
At our struggle
And he was quiet,
ever thoughtful,
On the way home, in the sand.
There was not much to say, after my day
After our year
So we were quiet.

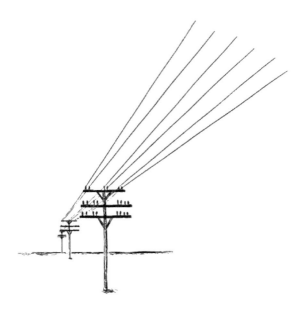

# with fever

churning and slick
my stomach
cannot digest your face
or voice
or wrist
or ankle

# First Love

I have loved all my life
As the sun shone through the leaves
bathing me in green
and the flowers in my hand, so delicately tied.
I have loved the wings that carry birds and
butterflies
The ones that now fill my stomach
as a new love finds me
through the gray haze of approaching summer
rain.
I give in to your lovely stain
I tie myself to your chain
And now I wait.

# Point of No Return

Taken from me, is the innocence
of backyards in the winter
When cold was just snow on the ground
not an icy heart turned bitter

But I watch my butterflies flicker
into smudges of red on paper
and it's you I now see in their wings,
it's to you that I am tethered, and I wonder
how I got here in this
mess of shattered glass-
The light that it once held now gone
with the hope that it would last

I am broken like that window
I'm as colorless as your face
that you hide in pits of self-despair
in which I now am traced, and they're unfazed
while I drag my feet in a daze
Color gone, the veil now drawn,
the things I love, now things distracting
just so I don't drown in hate, but

I feel the walls restricting, I
see it solidifying, the
barrier distancing me from
before, this is the after, and
I reach but I can't grab it, now I
grieve and I can't stop it, but the
rush of life continues, though
somewhere along the line-
I lost the point and how to find it,
in someplace with my mind.

Wake up
You urge me
You nudge me where I lay
Wake up
Wake up
Wake up
Wake up
Wake up
Wake up
Wake up

# Over the Line

It does not feel quite possible
to believe in the sun
as it rises over the line
So far away

It does not feel quite possible
to believe in the birds
that still sing in the morning
Before everyone awakes

It does not feel quite possible
that my skin still warms
from the light that appears over the line
That is so far away

Yet while I cannot feel
the possibility of anything
I hear your voice
Calling me to stay
Anyway

# Rattling Souls

Oh to take a deep breath
And not feel the rattle of a loose soul
Made alien in internal depth
Yet when without, maddeningly unwhole.
But simplicity is lovely
They say ignorance is bliss
Misplacing one's soul can testify to this

And if darkness could pass by
without a scratch on my side
within the dust and cover of misery's leather hide-
If breath could rise without feeling a rattle,
and love wasn't a disease, a woe to my core,
If the lungs didn't rasp in an unseen battle,
and the promise of peace did not require war-
The burden of a soul would not be sensed or tried
Its weight a golden feather,
a sparkling yellow lie.

How to see but not feel unowned pain?
How to carry but not take the weight?
Love is a gift and hate only takes
Why a line so blurry to separate?

# Midnight Musing

With the night comes merrily skipping thoughts
Hand in hand over beaming, moonlit sheets;
Walking down streets of what should be
forgotten
Proudly quickening my dreading heartbeats.
Out the window stays life's silent echoes
With the sky, darkened by a million closed eyes;
One pair will stay open, wishing for yellows
Awaiting relief from the golden sunrise.
If only those thoughts, now lovers with night;
Those thoughts so taken by stillness, such bliss,
Would instead fall in love with morning light
And leave this tired soul a goodnight kiss;
It wouldn't be such a trouble to sleep
But rather, will night's rich slumber stay deep.

# Renovation

Sometimes I see your lines
in the darkness of the night
on the arms of the ones I love
and the whisp in my bathroom mirror

I find you in the walls
walking down memory halls
Reaching out to pick peeling paint,
I feel the ache of renovation

A pain is in my ear
Though my eyes are getting clear
And I see the sun that rises
Realizing I do not dread it.

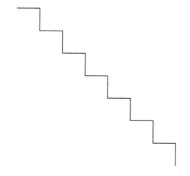

# The Only Reason

There is something about living-
like laughter is worth having
and dreams are worth chasing-
that dissolves into nothing,
like the water in my blood
that will one day become the earth,
along with walks under the moon
and stolen kisses by the gate
after watching waves that crash
onto rocks that never change,
unlike the scars on your hands
which I now face,
different than the others
because it was with love
that you surrendered openly
to give a reason for it all.

# Onward

The tendency of time
Flutters forward, sure and slow
Now tied by promise instead of rope
And the bruises start to fade.

# Return of the Butterflies

Strength did not find me
until the butterflies came flying
in all colors
with the thunder
And it began to rain.

Together we hid in leafy
shadows
comforted by the grassy pillow
watching the rain
as it cleaned
And we began to talk.

Their wings coated my arms,
conversation bringing a new dawn
of understanding
and forgiving
And whispered dreams of the future.

Strength
Is finding beauty once again.

# Sincerely,

It is with hope that I close
Though the seal will be left open
For more colors to be written
As life continues to move
For the purpose of none but you,
Creator of Good,
And all things beautiful.